This is a draft copy of:

Off Road Parenting

Caesar Pacifici, Ph.D.
Patricia Chamberlain, Ph.D.
Lee White

Please makes notes of errors you
may find in this book, and let us
know how we can improve it.

Notes:

_____

_____

_____

_____

_____

_____

_____

_____

_____

_____

_____

_____

_____

_____

_____

_____

_____

_____

_____

Please make notes, tear out this page, and send to:
Northwest Media Inc., 326 W. 12th Ave., Eugene, OR, 97405

Published by Northwest Media Inc., Eugene, Oregon

Off Road Parenting

Published by:

 Northwest Media, Inc. ■ 326 West 12th Avenue ■ Eugene, Oregon 97401
phone: 541-343-6636/fax: 541-343-0177
e-mail: nwm@northwestmedia.com
Web address: www.northwestmedia.com

Book design and jeep illustrations by Diane Cissel

Cover illustration by Jan Eliot
Stone Soup cartoons by Jan Eliot

Printed in the United States of America
ISBN 1-892194-25-2

Table of Contents

About the Cartoons

The cartoons sprinkled throughout this book were selected from a syndicated comic strip, *Stone Soup*, created by Jan Eliot. The blended families of *Stone Soup* are a great example of an "off road" family.

Stone Soup centers on the life of a single mom, **Val**, with her two daughters, hormone-filled pre-teen **Holly** and 9-year-old **Alix**, and Val's sister, **Joan**, who is in a second marriage with a loving guy named **Wally**. **Grandma**, who is full of wisdom, lives upstairs. Add to that, continuous step-child conflicts, Wally's kinship care of a rescued teen nephew, **Andy**, and Joan's hyperactive two-year-old son, **Max**, and **Biscuit**, the family dog.

Full of surprises, angst, anger and love, the goings on of this comic strip family are enough to make real families laugh at some of their own goings on. Read on and you'll probably count your-self among the many who already love the *Stone Soup* family.

Introduction

"Off Road Parenting" is just a way of saying that no matter what obstacle or breakdown you encounter on rough roads, you need to be prepared to use your tools to keep you going.

I s parenting like driving off-road? Parents often find themselves in unfamiliar territory with their children, trying to clear obstacles. And doesn't it always seem to happen just when you think things are going smoothly? But parents, like off-road drivers, can draw on their experience and tools to get back on track.

Whether you are raising a foster, adopted or birth child, this approach will give you those tools as well as some positive experiences in changing problem behavior. The book describes the basic tools you will need to accomplish this. The DVD gives you the opportunity to practice using these tools with realistic video stories of family situations. Together, they will help you find solutions to problems and build your sense of confidence in doing so. All in all it's designed to make parenting more enjoyable!

This book really shouldn't exist. Normally, publishers would not spend the money to produce training as complex as this. But thanks to a Small Business Innovation Research grant from the National Institute of Mental Health, we were able to undertake this project. Over the last two years, we've worked hard to write a book that is easy to read and to produce interactive video stories that are true to life.

This product is a first-of-a-kind in self-help parenting books. The realism of the video stories and the ability of the viewer to direct the stories to different outcomes is about as close as we can bring you to real life parenting situations.

Although our specialty is foster and adoptive parenting, we think *Off Road Parenting* will be just as useful to birth parents, stepparents and other family members who deal with difficult behavior problems.

Overview

Children's behavior sometimes requires more serious attention. But, that doesn't have to include actions that are hurtful, such as hitting, humiliating or yelling. Effective discipline only has to give children the message that their behavior was a problem. If a negative consequence is used, it should be so light that it can be used several times a day without causing harm.

While some parents may overreact to their child's misbehavior, other parents may be so unsure about disciplining their child that they don't act at all. Being able to use discipline is part of being a good parent. When done effectively, and in a home atmosphere that is upbeat and positive, discipline works.

Sorting Out Behavior

One way of looking at children's behavior is to sort it into two types: desirable behavior and undesirable behavior. Knowing how to respond to both is equally important. Letting children know when their behavior is desirable helps build their self-esteem.

Undesirable or disruptive behavior can come from many sources, including a natural need to rebel and test limits, a learning disability, poor social skills or a traumatic life event. Disruptive behavior isn't only "acting out" behavior, like yelling or hitting. It can also be "hidden" behavior, like stealing, vandalism or inappropriate touching. Not all hidden behavior is serious; it can be as simple as nail-biting or stashing food. Hidden behavior is harder to pin down, and so it may be harder to change.

This book stresses that disruptive behavior, whether it's acted out or hidden, can be changed, whatever a child's age.

Reaching Out

This book is not the single source for answers on managing

child behavior. Talk to other parents about parenting. When the going gets tough, the tendency is to turn inward and avoid other people. Don't do it — isolation is the enemy of all parents. Force yourself to get out of the house and have some free time to be with people and talk things out. Join an organized group or participate in a playgroup, so your child can get together with other kids and you can get to know other parents. Anything that puts you in contact with other parents who want to talk about problems and ideas will help ease frustrations. You can bet you're not alone.

Change does take time and effort, so give new parenting tools a chance to work. If this approach doesn't seem to be helping in say a month or two, talk to professionals whom you trust. There are some suggestions on how to choose a helping professional in the last chapter.

Chapter 1

Stuck

Sometimes when I'm stuck in bumper-to-bumper traffic, sitting in my 4x4, I look at that grassy center divide and think how easy it would be to break loose and get to where I'm going.

It's up to you to stop a child's disruptive behavior. Left unchecked, it can dominate life at home. But sometimes, as many parents discover, when you try fixing a problem behavior, it actually gets worse. What can you do? Can you really afford to ignore it? Our answer is simple: Instead of trying to change a child's behavior, start by changing yours, and, in most cases, his positive behavior will follow.

This book gives you the skills to change how you respond to a problem behavior, whether you're just starting to deal with one, or it feels like you're at the end of your road. By changing the kind of attention you give a problem, it will move your focus from the problem to the solution. This isn't always easy to do, especially with older children, but the payoff is great.

Frustration sets in when a child won't cooperate. It makes his relationship with you, his teachers and other kids tense. It's also frustrating for him, because it doesn't bring him what he really wants: love and acceptance. Over time, a vicious cycle begins. You ask him to do something, but he doesn't mind you. That makes you mad, so you insist. Well, that only makes him want to defy you even more. It becomes a battle of wills where everyone is throwing fits. With every growing demand to cooperate, he becomes less likely to comply. What's worse, you both end up feeling bad about yourselves.

The problem could start with something as simple as asking him to put on his shoes or take out the garbage. Instead of agreeing, he does anything he can think of to get out of it. He may ignore you, whine, argue, cry, throw a tantrum, even storm out of the house, slamming the door twice to make sure you get the point.

Even though this kind of behavior would be upsetting to any parent, parents sometimes do the same things. They whine, cry, yell or hit children, all in an attempt to get them to behave. The fight can leave parents shaken and confused, wondering how a little request could blow up into such a big battle.

Who's the winner when this happens? Is it the frustrated parent or the child who has learned that:

🌟 He doesn't have to take out the garbage – at least this time?
🌟 He can win a battle?
🌟 He can get your full attention by upsetting you?
🌟 He can train you to stop asking him to do things by making it worse next time?

As these fights continue, each one worse than the last, you both try to control each other's behavior by becoming more and more negative. But sooner or later, your determination to win the next battle finally falls apart, and now you're really stuck in the mud.

That is a defining moment. By giving up, you've unintentionally taught him that bad behavior can result in avoiding responsibilities around the house. And he's taught you that if you stop asking him to do things, you don't have to fight. He has taken emotional control of the household.

Less obvious, but more damaging in the long run, is the fact that he's not learning the key skills he needs to get along in his world. Taking out the trash may not sound like a life-shaping event, but everyday living skills are the foundation of self-sufficiency and self-worth.

Unstuck

When a child tries to push your buttons and you don't react the same old way, he will see you in a different light. You will surprise him, and he will take notice. He will grow to respect you for taking back control, and he will start to see the benefits of changing his own behavior. He begins to learn cooperation – a key ingredient to becoming a successful adult.

Chapter 2
Teaching Cooperation

They say the only reason
people have 4X4s is to
get stuck harder and
in worse places than a
regular car.

To get along in life, children of all ages have to learn to cooperate. Cooperation takes two critical skills: listening and following directions. These are the necessary ingredients for getting along with parents, teachers and friends.

Teaching cooperation starts at home with everyday tasks. By learning to cooperate, your child will build self-confidence. A child who works well with others gets praised, and praise feels good. A confident child is a child who is willing to learn new skills, get along with others and do her best in life.

70 Percent

It's easy to make sweeping statements that a child never minds you or always acts up. That's your frustration talking. Let's face it – she is not going to cooperate all the time. That's not realistic. Research shows that if she cooperates 7 out of 10 times, the stress is manageable. Somehow, 70% seems to be the magic number. If she cooperates less often than that, it feels as if she is constantly defying you. That's when your stress can start to spiral out of control.

Quick Check on Cooperation

Your expectations often can get in the way of seeing what's really going on with a child's behavior. The Quick Check on Cooperation form in the back of this book will help you do just that: get a quick check on how much of the time she cooperates at home.

Here's how it works: Choose a time of day when you can be together with her for about an hour straight. During that time, make some typical requests. For example, tell her to do one of her chores or something helpful; or if she is acting up, make a request about changing her behavior.

Don't make too many requests, or unusual ones. Keep it low key. For each request you make, if she started to mind within about 10 seconds after your first request, then check that she cooperated. If she did not, then check that she did not cooperate.

Do this for two or three days in a row.

To find out how much of the time she cooperated, divide the total number of times you made a request by the total number of times your child minded. You may be pleasantly surprised!

You can watch examples of this in Chapter 2 of the DVD.

Making Effective Requests

Teaching your child how to cooperate may mean making some changes in how you ask her to do things.

She can't be expected to cooperate if she doesn't know exactly what you want. Sometimes parents complicate things by getting too worked up when asking for help. At other times, requests are too vague or confusing. Keep it simple. You can avoid an argument.

Here are four steps to making an effective request:

1. Get Her Attention

Kids of all ages sometimes have a hard time staying focused. If you can get her attention, it will be harder for her to ignore you. Later on, she can't say she didn't hear you or understand what you meant. Here are some ideas: gently touch her shoulder; say her name to get her to look at you. A small child may not pay attention until you stand close to her and look her in the eye.

2. Be Calm

Don't expect a fight before it happens, even if past battles are still fresh in your mind. If you ask her to do something with anger in your voice, it will make her angry, too. Then she may not even hear your request, and once again, the battle is on. Keep your voice steady and calm.

3. Be Specific

Give just one direction at a time to make sure she understands you. Breaking down household jobs into small steps is one way to do this. For example, feeding the dog can be broken down into four tasks: finding the dog's dish, pouring the dog food, putting the dish on the floor and closing the dog food bag.

To make sure she understands the request, have her repeat it. If it's not clear, you can rephrase it. This simple step shows consideration and can save a lot of hassles later.

If you say, "Do you want to take a bath?" you are inviting a refusal. In this case, it is better to just ask for what you want. Adding her name before a request always adds a nice feeling to it, too: "Erika, it's time to take your bath now."

Parents often ask their kids to clean their room. That means different things to different people. Some families expect the room to be spotless; others just want the toys put away. The request may be too vague and too complicated, especially for very small children. Parents may need to stay with kids to show them exactly what they want. That is called "modeling," or showing how to behave. It's the most powerful teaching tool parents have.

4. Encourage Cooperative Behavior

Give encouragement when she's done what you've asked. It can be a hug, a thank you, or earning points toward a reward. (There's more on using encouragement in Chapter 4.)

Positively Magic

When the pot's boiling over on the stove, the dog's chasing the cat and the kids are all demanding attention, it's easy to fall back into old patterns of communication. On the **left** are some examples of ineffective ways parents make requests; on the **right** are examples of clearer, more positive ways to make those requests.

Ineffective	Effective
Why can't you pick up after yourself?	Please pick up your jacket.
Do you have to throw that there?	Put the book in your room.
Do you call that bed made?	You forgot to pull the sheet up.
Use your manners.	Please wait until your mouth is empty before talking.
Can't you see that's a mess?	Please put your clothes away.

When you give a child good directions, she can better understand what she is being asked to do. With the right kind of guidance, she learns to cooperate. This is pleasing to you, and it makes her feel more confident and willing to try new things.

Tips for Different Age Groups

2-6 Years

Simply calling a young child's name probably won't get her attention. Crouch down to get on her level, look her in the eyes and give just one instruction that she can easily understand. Also, if you are physically near her, rather than across the room, you can speak in a soft voice. A hug afterward will show her that good things happen when she cooperates.

7-12 Years

You may want to wait till a break in the TV show, or you may need to turn off the TV or computer to redirect a child's attention. Do it calmly, and stay calm when making your request. Keep it simple, and don't forget to praise her efforts.

13 Years and Up

Do not resort to name calling or saying things like, "you never...," or "you always...." Be direct and clear. Once the task is completed, an encouraging word will boost a teen's self-confidence.

Chapter 3
Tracking Behavior

Driving back roads
without a map or a
GPS is lots of fun
until you want to
go home.

When a behavior problem goes unchecked, frustration can quickly take over. And when you're frustrated, it tends to blur your understanding of what's going on with a child and what to do about it. You can hear the frustration when parents sometimes say, "He just yells all the time," or, "He doesn't sit still for a minute," or, "He's out of control." This chapter describes "tracking," a technique that will help you step back and get a clearer picture of a child's behavior. This can give you a practical starting point for communicating with him about his behavior.

Accentuate the Positive

No matter how much trouble kids can cause, they all have strengths and abilities that can be admired and praised. It's always a good idea to remind yourself of these, especially before trying to tackle a problem behavior. So before getting into tracking, take a little time to write down some of these qualities. Make a list of 10 great things about your child: Does he help in the kitchen? Is he kind to younger children? Is he creative? Athletic? Sometimes the very quality that you see as problematic can also be a strength. For example, if he is strong-willed, it is understandable that this can be challenging to you. Fortunately, the same quality can also signal positive attributes, such as an ability to lead or to see projects through to completion.

How to Use Tracking

Tracking behavior is not a punishment. It isn't spying, either. Tell your child, using words he can understand, that you are going to watch his behavior, because you want to learn how to fix a problem and to reward him for good behavior. The Tracking

Behavior form in the back of this book will help you do that. You can get a better understanding of tracking by watching Chapter 3 on the DVD.

Tracking involves three steps:

1. Pick a problem behavior.

You know your child best and what behavior of his is a problem. Start by picking one that you want to work on.

Once you have chosen a problem behavior, think of its opposite. What would his behavior look like if the problem didn't occur? For example, if he often uses a very loud voice when he plays inside, then the opposite would be that he speaks at an appropriate volume in the house. Don't leave out this step. It's just as important to track good behavior as it is to track problem behavior.

Also, make sure you pick a behavior, not a feeling. For example, you may say that you don't want a child to be so angry. But anger is a feeling, not a behavior. And he probably can't help it if he feels angry. It's healthy to express a feeling, but not through negative behavior. When tracking, look for the behavior, not the feeling. That is something you can change without denying his feeling.

For example, does he hit his sister when she tries to take his toy? It helps to ask yourself, "What does the problem behavior look like or sound like?" Some other feelings or characteristics that are not behaviors are laziness, irritability, jealousy and irresponsibility. For each of these, find the behavior you want to change or encourage.

2. Pick a time.

Set aside about an hour when you can watch his behavior. Make it a time when he's active and the problem behavior is likely to show up. If the behavior happens when he plays with his sister, then choose a time when they usually play together. Keep in mind also that you'll need to do this at the same time for at least 3 days in a row.

3. Track the behavior.

As you watch the behavior during these 1-hour sessions, your job is to keep track of how many times the problem behavior occurs and how many times the opposite — the good behavior — occurs. Using the Tracking Behavior form in the back of this book, write down each time either one happens.

For example, if you are tracking yelling, break the hour up into 5- or 10-minute periods. If he didn't yell during the first 5 minutes, then write down that he spoke in an appropriate voice during that period. But if he yelled, then write down that he yelled during that period. Repeat this for the next 5-minute time period, and so forth, until the hour is up.

Another type of problem you can track is minding — whether he follows your requests. If you choose to work on this, make sure it's during a time that you make several requests. Then write down when he minded and when he didn't mind.

Whatever behavior you see during these tracking sessions, respond to him the way you normally would. The idea is just to see how often the behavior happens. After keeping track for at least 3 days in a row, count how many times the problem behavior occurred and how many times the good behavior occurred.

Tracking: Is It a Good Thing?

Some parents are going to feel that, in their situation, the pen is definitely not mightier than the sword. All this business of watching and writing about a disruptive behavior can seem abstract. But tracking is indeed a very effective technique. It will help you understand how to set limits on undesirable behavior, on the one hand, and encourage good behavior, on the other hand.

Here's why you should use tracking:

🌟 Instead of fueling the feeling that the behavior is happening all the time, you'll know how often it really happens, and that alone can relieve a lot of frustration.

🌟 As you watch the behavior, you also will learn more about it. For example, does the behavior happen in some circumstances but not others? Perhaps you notice that he gets upset about sharing his toy because his sister teases him about it. Or maybe you notice that he gets increasingly revved up as dinner approaches, because you're busy preparing it, and he doesn't have adequate supervision or a structured activity that would occupy his attention. If that's the case, then it can change your understanding of what the problem is.

🌟 You will have a better understanding of what good behavior you want to replace the problem behavior. This will help you change your response to the problem behavior. Instead of telling him to stop ignoring you, tell him to answer you in 10 seconds. Now if he hits his sister, you can tell him to keep his hands to himself while he plays, rather than yelling at him to stop hitting. If your 5-year-old is whining, don't tell him to stop whining, tell him to speak in his 5-year-old voice. "Don't throw the toy truck" can become, "roll the truck on the floor."

✿ Each time you notice him doing the right thing, it is a golden opportunity to encourage that behavior. Thizs moves the focus of your relationship with him away from the frustration of problem behavior and toward the pleasure of encouraging good behavior.

Tips for Different Age Groups

2-6 Years

Track behavior during a routine like getting ready for bed or for preschool. If you're tracking minding, it's best to make requests during one-on-one time.

7 Years and Up

Introduce tracking in a positive way. Avoid lecturing or nagging about his behavior when you're tracking it. Let him know how he's doing. Show him the tracking form and try to use pictures.

Chapter 4

Encouragement

There is nothing more comforting when you're stuck than to know that you can simply shift into 4-wheel drive to get your car — or your-self — out of a ditch.

Encouraging good behavior not only makes it happen more often, it makes everyone involved feel better. When children feel success with one skill, they gain the confidence and courage to try new ones. But it takes the right kind of encouragement, given at the right time, to make it work.

Your Personal Philosophy

Some parents grew up in households where they didn't hear a lot of encouraging words. Others were raised to believe that children shouldn't be encouraged often, especially for doing something that is already expected of them, like their homework. You wouldn't expect to hear them say something like, "Carlos, it's great to see you already completed your homework. Let's break into the ice cream."

If you didn't get a lot of encouragement as a child, you may find it more difficult to give it to a child. Take a moment to think about these questions. They may help you put into perspective your beliefs and attitudes about giving encouragement.

- How much was encouragement a part of your upbringing?
- Do you use encouragement with your child?
- If that is different than your own upbringing, what made you change?
- How do you feel when someone encourages you?

What Is Encouragement, Anyway?

Encouragement can come in many forms. Sometimes it can be praise — a simple "Good job!" Other times, kids need more than a kind word. It may take a hug, a special treat or giving more of your attention by playing Legos or going to the park. There are hundreds of ways you can encourage a child.

Whether you encourage with praise, attention or a certain reward, it should convey a positive and personal message. There are three types of messages that have proven to be especially effective when encouraging children:

* *"You can do it,"*
* *"You have good ideas"* and
* *"You are important."*

Of course, you don't have to use these exact words. Say it in a way that is clear, simple and sincere. Be sure to check out Chapters 4 and 5 in the DVD.

Here are some tips on how to do this:

Look him in the eye.
Stop what you're doing and speak directly to him.

Be specific.
Tell him exactly what makes you happy. Instead of saying, "You're a good boy," say, for example, "I really like it when you put away your toys."

Praise often.
Use praise whenever you notice him doing something positive.

Praise immediately.
Don't brush him off because you're busy. Effective praise can take as little as 2 seconds!

Show enthusiasm.
Use a smile, a gentle touch or a hug to show your appreciation. Actions speak as loudly as words.

Be consistent.
The more consistently you encourage, the more consistently you will see good behavior.

Missed Opportunities

You can sometimes take positive behaviors for granted. For

example, it may seem uneventful when he plays quietly or puts away a toy. Because these are the types of behaviors you want to increase, don't miss the opportunity to encourage them as they happen. Some other positive behaviors to watch for include being polite, trying something new, sharing, getting an idea, using manners or being creative.

Don't be afraid to jump in and say something encouraging when you see a good behavior. Maybe you worry that if you stop him when he's playing quietly, he'll remember to be bad. But all it takes is a quick recognition of good behavior to encourage it — perhaps a thank-you or a smile that shows you notice it.

Putting Encouragement Into Action

Here's an example that shows how to put encouragement to work.

Mike and Janet would love for their 10-year-old son, Steve, to be more responsible about his homework assignments. They know he is a bright boy; his teachers say so, but they also say that his homework assignments are poor. He's failing most of his subjects.

They tried buying Steve a new desk and setting up a time for him to study, but that didn't work. Then they started giving him extra chores to do when he didn't finish his homework. That didn't work either.

In fact, rather than working harder, Steve started to lie. He told his parents that he didn't have any homework. They knew it wasn't true, but they didn't know what to do.

Mike and Janet had some good ideas about motivating Steve to do his homework, but they were still concentrating on what Steve wasn't doing, instead of looking for positive behaviors that he was doing. So they changed their strategy.

Mike and Janet began by tracking Steve's behavior just after he got home from school, when he's supposed to do his homework. They noticed that he usually sits down for a little while but then quickly gets distracted. They started giving him praise when he sat at his desk. If he opened his assignment book, they rewarded that, too.

Mike and Janet are letting Steve know that they notice and appreciate the effort he is making. Still, changing Steve's behavior can take time. They have to be flexible and keep their expectations realistic. Even if using encouragement doesn't solve their problem right away, it will probably make the atmosphere at home much more positive.

Timing Is (Almost) Everything

Rewards work well when you give them just after a child does the behavior you want. If one-on-one time with Dad is used as a

Here are some ideas for rewards to encourage positive behavior.

You probably already use many of these during your normal everyday time with your child. What makes these effective rewards is giving them right after a positive behavior.

Privileges

- Choosing a special TV program
- Getting first dibs on bathroom in morning
- Attending a special event (party, dance)
- Getting extra time on the telephone with friends
- Having a friend over for the evening or to spend the night
- Staying up half an hour later
- Watching cartoons
- Visiting with a special family member
- Going to a friend's house to play
- Taking bottles to the store and keeping the deposit refund
- Using Mom's makeup

Parent Time

- Playing a board game
- Taking a walk
- Going to a movie
- Going to the park
- Baking or cooking
- Going for ride on the motorcycle
- Working on a craft project

Rewards that Cost Money

- Nintendo or other TV game
- Trip to the swiming pool or skating rink
- Comic book
- Clothing
- Books
- Grab bag of fun small items wrapped up

Food

- Dried fruit
- Popcorn
- Special dinner, lunch or dessert
- Pizza
- Gum

Keep It Interesting

There is no single type of encouragement that will work in every situation or with every child. When you find one that works, don't wear it out. Children stop responding to a reward when they get bored with it.

reward for studying, it is most effective if that can happen the same day the child earns it. If that's not possible, then acknowledge that he earned a reward. Or if you want to give the reward, for example, only after he studies four out of five nights, keep track by giving him a star on a chart and let him know he did a good job. It's always good to be prepared and have a reward in mind — perhaps even making a list of possible rewards.

Here are some ideas on how you can schedule rewards:

Daily Rewards

If a child is under 7 years, rewards should closely follow the behavior. With older children, you can gradually delay giving a reward until later in the day. If a child, for example, played without throwing a tantrum, he can get reward stickers, a box of raisins or be allowed to stay up 10 minutes past bedtime.

Weekly Rewards

A weekly reward could be earned with five stars marked on that week's calendar. He could earn a poker chip or coupon for every day of good behavior. Those could be turned in for a reward at the end of the week.

Cumulative Rewards

Rather than requiring a good behavior five days in a row, you may find that he does better if you give a reward after he does the behavior five times. That way, even if it takes him 2 weeks to earn a reward, he will still succeed.

The Costs and Benefits of Rewards

Rewards have some cost, either in money or in time and effort. Before deciding on a reward, think about what the behavior change you want is worth to you. Is it worth 15 minutes of your time? Is it worth a small amount of money?

Rewards become more meaningful when a child can help

choose them and how to earn them. For example, if he wants a new video game, he can earn it by doing his chores every day for a couple of weeks. Or you may agree to give him $2 a week for the chores, with the idea that he can save the money toward buying the new game. Long-term goals need to be supplemented with daily rewards as well.

Don't promise more than you can afford. Don't promise time you don't have. Don't promise a reward that you feel is bigger than a child's efforts. Encourage him to do well and reward him for it. The plan doesn't work if you are not happy about giving the reward. It creates unhappy feelings and does nothing to improve the atmosphere at home.

Problems With Rewards

Children outgrow certain rewards quickly. A toy that was all the rage one week may fall out of favor the next. Even using the same phrases, such as "good job" or "great" can grow old and lose their effect. Stay in tune with children's changing tastes and needs.

Some parents see rewarding kids as a form of bribery, but there is an important difference between bribery and rewards — or any type of encouragement. A bribe is given before the behavior, with the hope that it will then influence the child to do what you want. The problem with this is that he can quickly figure out how to get the reward without doing what he was asked to do. A reward is given only after he has done what you want him to.

Some kids may have a hard time accepting rewards or praise. They may even act worse after getting complimented. If they are not used to hearing praise, they may seem unaffected by it. Or they may be suspicious of praise, because they think there are strings attached; maybe they expect to be asked for a favor or affection as "payback" for the praise.

If direct praise is difficult, you can praise a child indirectly. Talk to someone on the phone about how well he's doing when he can overhear. Write a note saying, "Good job on your room," or, "You were excellent sharing your new toy with your cousin," and leave it for him to find.

Remember, it is a rare child who doesn't respond to praise, and it is certainly worth trying. Time after time, it has been shown that children respond to encouragement. Paying attention to good behavior, using praise and staying positive can lead your child to see the advantages in better behavior. Over time, a more peaceful household and a more confident child are the result.

Keeping It Straight When There's More Than One Child

Rewards and privileges work best when they acknowledge an individual child. This is important to remember if your family has more than one child.

You can learn to individualize rewards pretty quickly. For example, let's say you are at a baseball game with two children. One child may have to sit beside you while another child may have earned the right to venture farther away. Obviously, this depends on the ages and abilities of the children involved and the safety of the environment, but it shows how one child can get a reward without affecting the reward received by another child.

Another idea is to let one child earn the right to stay up 15 minutes later than the other children. Most children consider this a real privilege. It makes them feel special, and if that time is spent with you, it is highly motivating.

Children also enjoy earning rewards for the whole family or group. For example, your child may be rewarded with a video rental that the whole family can watch. This gives everyone the opportunity to thank him and reinforce his good behavior.

Any time one child is left out of an activity, remember that just being left out is punishment enough. You don't have to lecture him; and don't let the other children make fun of him or continue to comment on it.

Two Parents, One Message

When it comes to using rewards, it's easier on everyone if both parents are consistent. Not only do children usually behave better when they know what is expected of them, but there is also less conflict between parents when each understands what the other is doing.

However, if you want to use rewards and your spouse doesn't, go ahead and use them, but encourage your partner to pay attention to your child's successes. While children will learn new behavior faster if both parents are teaching the same thing, they can still learn if the lessons come from just one parent. Children are expert at figuring out what different adults expect of them and behaving accordingly.

The purpose of using rewards is to teach a child good behavior. No time spent rewarding and praising him will ever be wasted. Your time with him will be more pleasant, and he will learn new behaviors that will help him get along better in life.

Tips for Different Age Groups

2-6 Years

Young children are so interested in pleasing their parents that simply telling them you are happy with their behavior can go a long way. Young children often misbehave dozens of times a day, so reward the good behavior as soon as you see it and as often as possible. The younger the child, the quicker the rewards should be given. Good rewards for this age group include hearing a story, going out to play or pushing the grocery cart.

7-12 Years

Pay attention to your child's good behavior, and it will quickly become clear that there is plenty to applaud — creativity, cooperation or a clean room. It's always better to give the praise or reward soon after the behavior happens, but if that's not possible, older children can work toward a reward. They can earn a coupon for every day of good behavior, for example, and redeem all their coupons for a reward at the end of the week. Rewards could be a homemade pie, a trip to the ice cream parlor or going to a friend's house to play.

13 Years and Up

Showing interest in a child will tell him he is important and boost his confidence, but if a teen hasn't heard a lot of praise, he may not respond well. Try encouraging him indirectly by praising him while talking to others. The rewards don't have to be immediate — they can be given after five instances of good behavior, for example. Rewards could include video rentals, additional telephone time or going fishing, shopping or out for pizza.

Chapter 5
Behavior Contracts

No matter how big the
obstacle blocking
the road, there is
usually a way to
get through it or
around it.

Making the Connection

To change behavior, it is important to connect a good behavior with a good outcome. Let's say a child washes the dishes, and you reward her by allowing her to watch a favorite TV program. She connects the desirable behavior with a positive outcome. Making this connection gives you a tool to promote good behavior, mostly through the use of rewards. Putting these connections to work is at the heart of the behavior contract.

Informal Contracts

When you tell a child, "After you make your bed, I'll fix a snack for us," you are not only making a connection, you are also setting up an informal contract. Think of it as a simple, short-term agreement. You probably use informal contracts pretty often. The good thing about an informal contract is that it connects a good behavior with a positive outcome. But for more difficult behavior, informal contracts may be too simple and short-term.

Formal Contracts

Children need a written plan to improve behavior. A good contract rewards a child for doing what's asked of her and lets her know exactly how she can succeed. Research studies show that this approach is remarkably effective. If a child cooperates, she gets the reward. If she chooses not to, there's no reward. Don't be too concerned if she doesn't get a reward. This approach puts the responsibility on her to change behavior. For you, it will be a welcome relief from anger and frustration.

The hardest part is writing the plan. Once that is in place, following it is relatively simple, even if she doesn't seem to care about pleasing you.

The beauty of a good contract is that you don't need to worry about why a child is more difficult than others. All you have to do is put the plan in place and stick to it. The only way to convince her that good behavior brings good things is to come through with a reward every time she succeeds.

Write It Down

A good contract helps you keep track of a child's good behaviors and the rewards she earns for doing what is asked of her. It works best if you first put it in writing. Here's why:

* It makes your life easier, because it's all spelled out — both the behavior and the reward.

* It gives the message that you are serious about what you're asking of her. If the contract focuses on what she is doing right, she'll focus on that, too.

* It sets goals and reminds her of the reward he can get if she does the task every day.

* It helps you pay attention to good behavior.

* It lets her know what is expected.

* It is non-emotional. There is no need for lecturing, nagging or explaining. It may be hard for you to turn these habits off. Just state what's expected, and she can either earn the reward or not.

* It allows you to track her behavior as well as your own.

Target a Behavior

In general, keep it simple for your first try. Start with one child,

not all of them, and start with just one behavior that seems relatively easy to fix. Remember to make sure it is a behavior you
want to change and not a feeling.

Here are some useful guidelines to follow:

Pick a simple behavior.

Don't try to change big problems, such as bedtime hassles,
skipped classes or public tantrums. It has to be obvious whether
it happens or doesn't happen. It can't involve any interpretation
or judgment call. For example, don't set up a plan to finish
homework, because you may not know about all the homework.
Instead, give a reward for spending a half-hour reading, studying
or doing homework.

Pick something that won't interfere with anyone else's chores.

For example, don't pick clearing the table if the table must be
cleared before another child can wash dishes. Instead, the chore
could be sweeping the floor after everyone else is finished in the
kitchen.

Pick something you're sure he can do.

For example, if she has hung up her coat in the past, but has
slacked off lately, pick that behavior. Other examples include
taking off her shoes when she enters the house, putting her
books in her room or taking her breakfast dish to the kitchen. It's
okay if the first few attempts at behavior contracts are easy
"giveaways." The idea is to teach her that she can succeed and
that success brings rewards. When you follow through with the
reward and lots of encouragement, she will like the whole
approach.

Make sure the behavior is broken down into steps she can understand.

Taking a breakfast dish to the kitchen could include picking up
the spoon and bowl, washing out the bowl in the sink and putting
the bowl on the counter.

Setting Up a Behavior Contract

The Behavior Contract form in the back of this book will help you organize writing a behavior contract with your child.

Here are the basic steps for creating a successful contract:

Fill in the child's name.
Make kids feel like they are a part of the process. Have them

fill in the information if they can. Maybe younger kids can just fill in their names. Try to use their words when you can.

Choose one behavior you want to encourage.

Make sure to include all the steps needed to complete the behavior. We made room for 5 steps, but you can use as many as you need. Notice, on the form we use the friendlier word "job," instead of "behavior" or "task."

Fill in the time when the behavior needs to be completed.

The time could be specific, for example 7 p.m., or more general, such as before dinner. The point is that she will know that, if she completes the job by the deadline, she will get the reward. Depending on her age or developmental level, you may want to give the reward just after the behavior is completed. If her job is to pick up her toys before dinner, the reward for completing it could be to help you make dinner or choose a dessert.

Fill in the number of times a behavior needs to be completed before a reward will be given.

It's reasonable for children to behave the way you want about 70% of the time. If they do a behavior four or five days out of the week, consider it a success. The decision on what it takes to earn a reward is yours, but remember that the idea is to help her succeed. You can always write into the contract a small daily reward that can be earned.

Decide on the reward before the contract begins.

Children need to know exactly what they are working toward. That's their motivation. Otherwise, it would be like having your paycheck depend upon your boss's mood or your most recent behavior. One idea is to discuss possible rewards with her and then give her two or three she can choose from at the end of the week. Don't give her one reward for 70% success and an additional reward for 100% success. Any suggestion that perfection is preferred puts too much pressure on her.

Mark successes on the chart.

For younger kids, use smiley faces or colorful stickers. For older kids you can just put check marks. Leave unsuccessful days blank. A blank space is negative enough. Do not draw a frown face. Remember to focus on the positive.

Additional Guidelines

These principles are crucial for success:

Reward every completed task in the contract.

No exceptions. Children get discouraged easily, and the smallest promise is very important. The main thing a behavior contract aims to teach children is that good behavior gets positive results. The best way to show them that good behavior is preferable is by delivering the promised rewards.

Stay involved in the program every day.

That means giving feedback every day and following through on the reward if one was earned. Children have short attention spans and need immediate gratification. There is no point in rewarding last week's behavior; children may not remember what they did or how they did it. An older child working for a long-term reward can also benefit from daily feedback that lets her know she is getting closer to earning her reward.

Write, draw or use materials at the child's level.

Stop yourself from getting too enthusiastic and writing a plan that's too complicated. It's plenty if a chart covers just one behavior, such as following directions. Use simple pictures, drawings or clippings instead of words. With a young child, the chart might include pictures of a bathtub, toothbrush and pair of pajamas, with room for a star to be placed beside each one when the task is completed. To see whether the plan is too complicated, explain it to your child, try it for a few days and ask her to explain it back to you.

Reinforce positive behavior and avoid punishment.

If earning a star will get her to brush her teeth, don't take away her favorite toy if she doesn't brush her teeth. Focusing on the positive will create a more pleasant atmosphere and teach her to learn good behavior more quickly.

The best way to know whether your incentive program is working is to look at her behavior. Re-evaluate the program about every 2 weeks to see whether the rewards are still reinforcing.

Presenting the Plan

With foster and adopted children, some may have had a bad experience with a contract in the past. For example, they may have been held accountable for behavior but not have received a promised reward. View the DVD to see ways to set up a contract. Here are some steps that will make it more likely for a child to accept a contract.

Set aside time to discuss the contract without distractions.

Present the plan one-on-one, just you and the child. This shows that you are serious about the process, and she can air her own concerns.

Find out if she's had other experiences with contracts.

You can skip this step if you already know that your foster or adopted child has had a bad experience with contracts. If she has, try to make it different by using a different type of chart or different words.

Talk about the good things she does.

Make a list of the behaviors you like. Then tell her that you sometimes lose track of all those positive behaviors and that she doesn't always get credit for them. Tell her that you are starting a new plan to give her more credit for good behavior.

Explain the contract.

Clearly state the behavior you want to see. Don't focus on the bad behavior. For example, you might say, "You know how I nag you all morning to get ready for school? Well, I'm sure you will be able to get ready without my nagging, so I'm not going to do it anymore. From now on, when you get ready for school on your own, you will get a reward." Describe each step you expect: eating breakfast, combing hair, putting shoes on and getting the backpack ready by 7:30. Write the steps down, or draw them, so she can refer to the steps each morning. Once the tasks are completed, give her a reward, one that she values.

Be direct. Don't leave room for negotiation. Instead of saying, "After school you can study, " say, "When you study for 40 minutes after dinner, you will get 15 points toward a reward." If she asks what happens if she doesn't study, tell her she won't earn any points.

Don't get discouraged if she is very resistant.

Do not let her sabotage the contract. It puts her in control. Even if she refuses to do what you've asked, calmly tell her that you are going to keep track anyway and that she will get a reward if she decides to do the chore or behavior on the contract. Then leave it alone. It is not productive to force a child to do a chore, but you can come up with a reward that might change her mind.

Be consistent.

It's important for all caregivers to participate. Even if one parent is primarily in charge of following the contract, the other parent at least needs to be supportive of the concept.

A written contract with clear goals and valued rewards works remarkably well. Your child quickly learns that the only way she can earn the reward is to follow the plan. You can work toward changing her behavior without confrontation.

Tips for Different Age Groups

4-6 Years

Two- and three-year-olds are too young for behavior contracts; just stick with giving them immediate rewards for positive behavior. Children 4-6 years old need to see a concrete connection between their good behavior and their reward, so they can remember to behave. Remember to give rewards right away for good behavior. When creating a contract, make it a simple and fun activity with your child by using pictures, drawings or clippings to show the tasks to be completed.

7-12 Years

As children get older, they can better understand a written contract, but it's still a good idea to focus on only one or two behaviors that are relatively simple. Decide on rewards ahead of time and always deliver quickly on your promises, or you will take away her incentive for good behavior. Give her feedback every day. Get her input as you write the contract.

13 Years and Up

Discuss writing the contract with your teen ahead of time. Keep your expectations realistic. Make sure she is capable of performing the tasks you ask of her, and remain flexible. Contracts for this age group should allow some room for negotiation. Rewards can now be given on a weekly or even longer-term basis, but continue to encourage her every day, so she can see that she's getting closer to receiving her reward. Stick with the plan even if she resists it.

Chapter 6

Troubleshooting Behavior Contracts

A small toolbox with the right tools is a lot more helpful in tough situations than a big toolbox with the wrong tools.

Self-Quiz

Behavior contracts work to change children's behavior, but they don't often work perfectly on the first try. Kids don't come through with their end of the agreement for a lot of reasons. At first, children may resist and test you. The problem behavior may actually get worse for a short time. But, if you have an effective contract, it will eventually work.

If the first plan you try doesn't work, ask yourself the following questions:

- Did you check the behavior every day?
- Did you give immediate feedback?
- Was the behavior broken down into small enough steps to understand?
- Did you encourage what was accomplished, even if he didn't finish the task?
- Did you provide the reward if it was earned?

- Were the rewards as worthy as the good behavior, and were they given soon after the task was completed?

- Did your spouse or other caregivers support using the contract?

- Did you use pictures and age-appropriate language in the contract?

- Did you set aside a time of day to review the contract with him?

- Did you show an interest in the contract by being positive and encouraging?

- Did you remain emotionally neutral when reviewing his performance?

- Was the contract the only way he could earn the reward?

- Did the contract require too much at one time?

Other Thoughts — Unintended Rewards

If a child keeps misbehaving, even after you've tried your hardest, it could be because he's getting something rewarding out of misbehaving. That something may not be obvious to him or to you.

Let's say you wrote a contract to be ready for the school bus by 8 o'clock, but it's just not working. It could be because he's getting rewarded for not getting to school on time. For example, when he is late to class, it might distract the teacher so that she doesn't ask him about the homework he didn't finish. Being late had a reward – he avoided the consequences of not finishing his homework, because the teacher didn't ask him about it. Or maybe he got to ride his bike to school, which he really likes.

Probably the most reinforcing reward you give a child is your attention. A child can find negative attention just as rewarding as positive attention. When you argue with a child, you're also giving him an unintended reward: one-on-one attention.

When you see that he is not responding to a reward that

ordinarily would be attractive, think about other kinds of rewards he may be getting from misbehaving. It's useless to ask a child why he keeps misbehaving. He probably doesn't see the unintended reward himself, and even if he did he wouldn't be able to explain it. This doesn't make him bad or manipulative. The reality is that kids are looking to get their needs fulfilled, but sometimes they go about it in unproductive ways. It is your responsibility to take on the job of figuring out how to help him respond to healthier rewards.

Tips for Different Age Groups

4-6 Years

One of the biggest challenges in using behavior contracts with young children is making sure they clearly understand the rules. Contracts should be simple. It should be obvious to the child that he has completed the task; and parents must follow through, delivering the reward every time.

7-12 Years

Even if a child doesn't complete his end of the bargain, use words to encourage any of his efforts on a daily basis. Simplify the contract if it seems too complicated, and make sure he understands that the only way he'll get the reward he wants is to follow the contract.

13 Years and Up

It's hard not to let your child influence your emotions if he refuses to follow the contract. Even if you understand the hidden payoff your child is getting from misbehaving, resist the temptation to explain his behavior to him. Stay calm and allow him to earn his reward if he follows through.

Chapter 7

Setting Limits

Sometimes the mud is so deep that no matter what 4x4 you're driving, you are going to need to be winched out.

Reaching the Limit

At some point, all parents have to set definite limits on their children's behavior. In spite of their protests, children need and want certain limits set. But not every kind of response is effective or even appropriate. This chapter helps clarify what kinds of limits work and what kinds don't work.

Ineffective Approaches

First, let's talk about some types of responses or limits that don't work very well.

Spanking or Hitting

Spanking or hitting may stop the misbehavior in the short run, but it has many long-term disadvantages:

🐾 It doesn't work.

Parents don't like spanking their kids. Plus, you can't spank a child every single time she misbehaves. The net result is that she gets away with misbehavior most of the time because you ignore it until you get mad enough to spank.

- **It shows parents have lost control.**
  This frightens children and makes parents feel guilty.

- **It sends a mixed message.**
  This is especially true if the behavior is hitting. It doesn't make sense for a parent to hit a child as a way to teach her not to hit. If a child sees a parent spanking to solve problems, she, in turn, learns to hit when she is frustrated. It gets passed from one generation to the next.

Harsh Discipline

Research shows that big punishments don't work. Parents can't deliver them every time a child misbehaves. Kids get confused, because sometimes they are punished and sometimes not. Kids don't need to suffer for discipline to be effective. They end up "hating" their parents when the discipline is severe.

Humiliation

Parents' anger and frustration sometimes come out in quick and humiliating remarks. What is said may not seem very important to parents at the time, but over time, it will scar a child's self-esteem.

Lecturing

Children tune out lectures. Actions work better. When you take action to deal with a behavior, do it calmly, unemotionally and with little talking. If children face consequences when they act up, it's the consequence – not the lecture – that will change behavior.

An Effective Approach: Setting Limits

There are much better options than spanking, harsh discipline, humiliation and lecturing to help children behave. The first step toward using any form of discipline is to set clear and firm limits.

The skills used in giving positive feedback are the same ones needed to set limits. You have to make clear requests; you have to deal with a child's behavior in an unemotional, objective way; and you have to follow through. For these skills, practice makes perfect.

House Rules

The limits you set for behavior should be based on rules you establish at home. Once again, the key is being clear and consistent. Many families have unwritten rules that are generally understood, such as flushing the toilet after each use, not throwing balls in the house and taking shoes off at the door. But some children need the rules to be spelled out for them, so make a list. Make the list brief, use age-appropriate and positive language, and communicate as much as possible with pictures, drawings or clippings.

Include only serious no-no's on your list of rules. Don't make the list too long or complicated, and don't put anything on the list that will not be followed up with a consequence. Good house rules should be about safety and respect for others.

Some examples:

Ask for permission before going into another person's room.

Tell your sister what you want instead of hitting her.

If you need help, ask Mom or Dad.

Knock on the bathroom door before entering.

Don't handle knives without asking.

If there is a rule you'd like everyone to follow, such as squeezing toothpaste from the bottom, but you don't want the hassle of enforcing it, leave it off the list.

A list of rules can make it easier for kids to see what behaviors will not be tolerated. Just as it was important for a child to understand what behavior will be encouraged, she must also understand which behaviors are unacceptable.

There are some good examples to see in the DVD.

Making the Rules Stick

What can parents do when kids don't abide by the rules despite their best effort? In the next three chapters, we will explore three kinds of effective discipline:

- time out,
- privilege removal and
- extra chores.

Each of these can be light enough to be used as many times as necessary each day, so that there is always a consistent consequence to the misbehavior. Even if it becomes necessary to use discipline, keep a positive tone. It will boost a child's confidence and stop you from getting into a negative rut. Don't forget to pay attention to the good behavior. Keep the encouragement and rewards coming, and changes in behavior will happen.

Tips for Different Age Groups

2-6 Years

Decide what behaviors – for example, hitting – are so unacceptable that you will immediately follow through with a consequence every time. Make sure a child understands that she will be disciplined if she violates certain rules.

7-12 Years

Tell your child what house rule is being broken. That will make it easier for her to know what behavior she is being disciplined for.

Be clear and direct about the rules and the consequences for breaking them, but keep your tone upbeat.

13 Years and Up

Resist the urge to lecture when the rules are violated. Stay calm, and remember that teens always need a boost of confidence and self-worth, so spend far more time highlighting positive characteristics you notice.

Chapter 8

Time Out

Kids are a lot like
4x4s, rough and
tough, but they
take a lot longer
to run out of gas.

Time out works best with children 2-12 years. They generally learn the procedure quickly and respond well. By 11 or 12 years, children start to resist it. Options such as removing privileges or giving extra chores work better with older children.

Out of Harms Way

Sometimes, when young children seriously act up, the situation has to be immediately stopped. Time out is an effective way to safely remove an out-of-control child from a situation for a brief time.

Children love attention, but when they're in time out, they don't get any. And if there's one thing children can't stand, it is not getting attention. This strategy accomplishes two important things: it physically removes a child from the immediate cause of his misbehavior, and it gives him the chance to calm down.

Time out also lets you stop the problem behavior from further escalating, and it puts an end to giving him attention for negative behavior.

Research shows that time out is most successful when the atmosphere at home is positive. That's why it is so important to remember to praise a child and be encouraging when he cooperates. If the home environment is not positive for him, he won't mind being removed from it. Under those circumstances, time outs don't work.

Preparing for Time Out

Select a place for time outs.

It should not be in an active part of the house. Find a place where he will not be stimulated by other interests. What works will vary from one child to another: it may be the bathroom, the mudroom, the laundry room; or maybe it's the enclosed porch that does the trick.

Prepare the time-out room.

Remove sharp objects, breakables, medicines or anything children can get into.

Decide how long time outs should be.

A good rule of thumb is to give one minute of time out for every year of age. Get a good timer with an alarm, and keep it handy.

Be consistent.

Children should understand exactly what behavior will land them in time out. They should know that the misbehavior will earn them a time out every time. Start with a simple behavior, one that you think you will have the most success in changing. Keep it to one behavior at a time, perhaps one you followed while tracking. Don't jump from one behavior to another.

Prepare him.

Let him know what will happen when he gets a time out. Show him where he will go for the time out, and show him the timer, too. That way, he knows what to expect.

Be ready to take a privilege away if he doesn't cooperate.

Decide in advance what privilege you will take away if he refuses to go into time out. More on this in the next chapter.

Time Out Guidelines

This is a great time to check out Chapter 8 on the DVD .

Setting it up.

🌀 Give warning.
You can give a child one warning if the situation is not yet out of control. Tell him matter-of-factly that unless he minds he will go to time out.

🌀 Commit.
Once you tell him he needs to take a time out, follow through, even if he completes the chore he just refused to do. You might say, for example, "Thanks for wanting to clean up now, but you didn't listen when you had the chance, so you still have to go to time out."

* **Label the problem.**
For example, say, "You didn't stop arguing. That's a time out." Or, "You didn't do what I asked. Go to time out."

* **Be calm and neutral when giving a time out.**
Act before you get angry.

* **Extend the time out if he refuses to take one.**
Remain calm. Every few seconds that he doesn't comply, say, "That's another minute in time out." Repeat this procedure until you get to nine minutes, then tell him a privilege will be taken away. For example, "That's nine minutes. If you don't go to time out right now, you can't ride your bike this afternoon."

* **Set a timer when he goes into time out.**
A timer works better than a watch, because children will listen for the timer to go off. It's a signal to both of you that time out is over.

Keeping it up.

Don't talk to him when he's in time out. Time outs are meant to remove him from social contact. Childproof the room, so you don't have to worry about him.

Ending it up.

Be consistent.

Whichever parent decided to give the time out should also be the one to bring him out of the time out.

Be done when it's done.

When the timer signals it's over, bring him out of time out. You don't have to ask him if he is ready or have him come out on his own. It should be business as usual. There's no need to lecture about the problem behavior or the time out.

Following it up.

Pick up where you left off.

Have him complete the chore he was asked to do before he went into time out.

Apply the same rules for time out if he still doesn't comply.

If he is still screaming or acting up, calmly tell him he is not ready to leave time out, and set the timer for two more minutes.

No apologies.

Don't apologize, and don't dwell on the bad behavior. Send the message that it's in the past.

Troubleshooting

The first few times you use time out, children may act like they are having fun. Don't worry; the novelty will wear off. You may even see an increase in misbehavior. This does not mean time out isn't working. It will work. Children will try to push your buttons to see how serious you are.

Here are some typical misbehaviors and reactions during time out:

Messes.

Kids can find a way to make a mess even in a child-proofed

room. Remain calm, and ask them to clean up the mess before leaving time out. If they refuse, you can extend the time out or take away a privilege.

Noisiness.

Children may protest by yelling or arguing, either before or during their time out. If so, try one of these three things:

1. ignore the noise, and consider it a success if they go into time out;
2. let them know that the time out doesn't start until they are quiet; or
3. tell them that it doesn't look like they are ready for a time out, and then take away a privilege.

I hate you.

He may feel as if he is pulling out the big guns to see how serious you are about time outs. Ignore this attempt to distract you from the misbehavior. Stay on track. Don't create an emotional situation.

Fine with me. I like time out.

Children often use this defense. Don't measure a time out's effectiveness by a child's reaction. Don't discuss the reaction. It drags out the process and leads to an unnecessary emotional exchange.

Stomping and muttering on the way to time out.

Ignore this. It's more important that he is going to time out. If the behavior gets worse, you can either ignore it or take away a privilege.

Frequently Asked Questions

What if my spouse will not use time out?

Consistency is important. Neither parent should not interact with the child during the time out.

What if my child says, "I don't care," or, "I like time out?"

Ignore those comments. Be confident that you are using an effective tool to change behavior.

What do I do when I feel too angry to give a time out?

If you feel angry enough to spank or yell, chances are that the situation has been going on for too long, and your frustration is at the breaking point. Intervening earlier can avoid this. Time out works better if it's done calmly and not combined with more harsh punishments.

What if my relatives feel I'm being too hard on my child when I send him to time out for a minor issue?

If he does not do what you say, it is not a minor issue. Let your relatives know you are not looking for advice.

What if my child misbehaves outside while playing with friends, and when he is told to go in the house for a time out, he refuses?

Give him the option of going inside for a time out or losing a specific privilege.

What if my child refuses to go to time out, so that I have to carry him there, shove him in and close the door real quick?

Don't get physical or even threaten it. If he refuses to go to time out, take away a privilege.

What if I have to use a time out away from home?

Make sure time outs work for you at home before you try them when you are away from home. Try making him sit in a quiet corner of a store, restaurant or church. At a sporting event or school function, the time out could be sitting beside you rather than moving around.

Is It Working Yet?

The only way to know whether time out is working is to see whether his behavior has changed. It doesn't matter what he says, even if he truly seems to enjoy time outs. The only thing that matters is whether the problem behavior starts to go away. Sometimes it happens slowly, so tracking will come in handy here. See how many times a day the behavior occurs. Over time, if time outs are used consistently, the behavior should decrease.

Wrong Direction

Frequently, the problem behavior will increase for a short time before it starts to decrease. This is normal. Be ready for it, so you don't get discouraged and give up. If you consistently show a child that you will not accept negative behavior, he will start getting the picture that you are serious.

Follow through when times get tough. Once you get past the brief episode, your job is nearly complete – at least for this behavior. Then it's on to the next!

Tips for Different Age Groups

2-6 Years

Keep time outs short – try 1 minute for each year of age – and don't feel you are being too harsh if you calmly use them throughout the day. Make sure he understands what he did wrong and the rules of the time out. Don't lecture him afterward. Let time outs speak for themselves. For children 2-3 years old, at first you can escort them to their time out.

7-12 Years

Pick just one behavior you want to change, and give a time out every time you see the misbehavior. Stick with your plan, and track the behavior to see if it's changing for the better. If not, consider taking away a privilege instead, as 11- and 12-year-olds may be especially resistant to time outs.

Quick Time Out Guide

Tell him:
- what he did wrong,
- that he needs a time out and
- how long the time out will be.

For example:
"That's a 5-minute time out for not minding."

If he doesn't cooperate, increase the time.

If he continues to refuse to go into time out after 9 minutes of assigned time out, take away a privilege.

Set a timer when he goes into time out.

When time outs don't work, you need to have a back-up plan — taking away a privilege. That's the topic of the next chapter.

Chapter 9
Removing Privileges

Trying to use a cell phone when you're in backcountry is like trying to talk with an angry teen: You just can't connect.

When to Remove a Privilege

Life is never simple. Just when you think you've got kids figured out, they change. Once you get your toddler's naptime routine down to 5 minutes flat, she'll decide she doesn't need naps anymore. The CD you bought your teen as a reward – so cool just last week – is now incredibly uncool.

It's the same with discipline. You can't always rely on the same old standbys. Many parents discover that, as their children get to be about 11 or 12, time outs begin to lose their effect. Preteens and teens hate it when no one pays attention to them, but the brief isolation of a time out doesn't feel nearly as bad as not having time on the telephone or not watching a favorite TV show. As children mature, removing a privilege can be a backup for time outs; eventually, time outs can be phased out.

As with any of the parenting tools in this book, removing a privilege works best when the atmosphere at home remains calm and positive. Be consistent, so a child learns that his world is not an unpredictable place, where he is punished for misbehaving one day but not the next.

Children need to know what to expect for both good and bad behavior. When a child earns a reward, she should get it every time. Similarly, when she violates a rule of the house, she should always get a consequence, such as getting a privilege taken away.

Using Privilege Removal

Decide ahead of time what privilege you will take away.
That way you don't have to think about it while she is misbehaving. Choose a privilege that she values, but don't make it excessive. Remember, what you take away is less important than the message you send – that there is a consequence to misbehavior.

Make sure the privilege is under your control.
For example, if you take away bike-riding time, make sure she doesn't have access to a bike.

Remove the privilege for no more than 1 or 2 hours.
Taking away a privilege for a long time doesn't work any better than a quick punishment. Besides, children resent harsh punishments, and they feel hopeless if they have to face an entire afternoon without privileges.

Follow through.
Keep your word when you say a privilege has been lost. She has to know that rewards and punishments are directly tied to his behavior.

Remove the privilege as soon as possible.
Get it over with. The sooner the discipline is over, the easier it is to restore a pleasant family atmosphere. For example, if she comes back very late after playing with her friends without calling you, remove something that evening, like TV time or dessert, rather than play time with friends the next day.

Don't remove a privilege that was earned.
She will lose her incentive for good behavior if earned rewards are taken away.

Troubleshooting

Taking away privileges may not go perfectly at first. Here are some guidelines to help you make some midcourse corrections.

Keep rewards separate from punishments.

Give her the rewards she has earned, even if you give her consequences for other misbehavior.

Don't punish yourself.

Don't ground her from a family outing if it means everyone has to stay home. Instead, restrict her from one part of the outing.

The family can still spend the day at the lake, let's say, but she can't go out in the boat or ride the Jet Ski.

Don't punish other children in the family.

If the other kids have earned a trip to the park, she could be told to help clean up later, or stick close to you rather than playing. Make sure she knows ahead of time that she will not be allowed to fully participate in the activity.

Don't take away something healthy.

Don't take away a sports activity if she's been cooped up in the house for a while because of bad weather. Don't take away computer time if she needs it to do schoolwork. Don't tell her she can't have visitors if she is shy and has difficulty making friends.

What if she doesn't mind me?

If she is defiant, you will have to take away a privilege that you can control completely. You control your money, so you can refuse to buy something she wants. You control your car, so you can refuse to take her where she wants to go. If you have to, keep treats locked in the trunk of your car. Do whatever you can to regain control, but make sure you are not confrontational or emotional. Don't, for example, push your way into her room and jerk a toy out of her hands. Remove the toys when she is not in the house. Do not get physical under any circumstances. Be smart. You ultimately have control over the "good stuff," so remove the privilege at your convenience.

Ideas on Privileges to Remove

* Television program.
  Just one program at a time.

* A favorite toy or game.

* Sports equipment.

* Time with friends.
  This could include playing outside with neighbor kids, having a friend over after school or having a friend spend the night.

🌸 Electronics, including stereo, radio or video games.

🌸 Telephone time.

🌸 Desserts or other special treats.

🌸 A family outing.

🌸 Usual bedtime. Make bedtime earlier.

Do you want to see how it's done? View it on the DVD.

Tips for Different Age Groups

2-6 Years

The same strategies used in giving time outs work for privilege removal, too. Take action just after she misbehaves, so she makes a clear connection between her behavior and the consequence. Don't just threaten to take away a privilege; follow through instead. At the same time, make sure she always gets the rewards she has earned.

7-12 Years

The most important thing taking away a privilege teaches is that misbehavior brings negative consequences. Don't get too hung up on what privilege to remove. Instead, focus on being consistent so she will learn, for example, that every time she's late for school she loses her skateboard privileges for that afternoon.

13 Years and Up

Act before you get mad. Take away the privilege for just an hour or two – long-term punishments don't work any better than short ones – and don't stew over the misbehavior. Get the punishment over with quickly to keep the atmosphere at home as positive as possible.

Chapter 10

Extra Chores

Even a 4x4 with studded
tires doesn't help
when you're going
too fast on an icy
road. If you can't
avoid being in that
predicament, don't hit the
brakes. Just keep your course, ease up on
the gas and make smooth corrections.

Regular Chore or Extra Chore?

Most kids have certain chores they do at home, such as washing the dishes or cleaning their room. An "extra" chore is different. It is given as a consequence for a negative behavior. It also has to be something that a child normally doesn't do, for example, if a pre-teen talks back rudely to you, and you have him do something extra, such as take out the garbage. Extra chores, just like regular chores, can be large or small, quick and easy or really, really boring. Chapter 10 on the DVD will show you what we mean.

When to Use Extra Chores

Extra chores are not for children under 7 years. For older children, an extra chore can be just as effective as removing a privilege in most situations. With extra chores, you're responding to misbehavior by adding something unpleasant; when you remove a privilege, you're taking away something pleasant. Whichever you choose, it's important to use it as soon after the misbehavior as possible. That way, he makes a clear connection between his behavior and the consequence. If, for example, you discover that your teen snuck out of the house and you decide to give an extra chore as a consequence, be sure to have him do it as soon as possible. At the very least, he should do it before he can have a next privilege, such as talking on the phone with his friends. In fact, tying an extra chore to a privilege is a doubly good strategy for insuring that the chore really gets done and that the connection between his behavior and the consequence is still fresh in his mind.

The most important thing about an extra chore is simply making that connection to the misbehavior. Try to match the severity of the chore to the seriousness of the misbehavior. If he did something relatively minor, such as not mind you when you asked him to turn off the TV, you might have him walk the dog or write down 10 different reasons minding is important. If he did something more serious, such as taking money from your wallet without asking, you might want to send him a stronger message and give him a tougher extra chore, like scrubbing the bathroom.

Extra chores and taking away privileges are also effective in situations where the problem behavior didn't just happen. For example, if he has been secretly taking and drinking alcohol from your liquor cabinet, an extra chore can still be an effective consequence, as long as you give it as soon as you discover the misbehavior.

Hidden Behavior

It's not unusual for kids to get into mischief that you don't know about. Sometimes, it's behavior they want to hide from you, and they may tell lies to cover it. If you find out that he took money from you without your permission, rummaged through your private possessions, shoplifted, committed an act of vandalism, hoarded food, or hit a sibling, it's probably not the first time he has done it. Most likely, it has been going on for some time and so it may be difficult to change. Don't change your basic strategy. When you discover the behavior, give him a consequence, whether it's the first or tenth time.

With hidden behavior you can't always be absolutely certain, or be able to prove, that a child did the behavior. If he lies about what he is doing, it can add more doubt. Don't worry about getting rock-solid proof. After some investigation, if you are reasonably sure "in your gut" that he was involved with something, go ahead and follow through with a consequence. Don't overreact, though. Treat the hidden behavior as calmly as you would any other misbehavior. Don't weigh down the problem with lectures about his moral values. Take action instead.

A great way to promote honesty is to reward it. Be careful not to confuse lying with storytelling in younger children. They are not the same thing. Children sometimes tell stories, because they blend or confuse facts and fantasy. If you aren't sure which is which, try asking if the story happened in his mind or in the real world.

With some behavior, once you discover it, you can take some preventive measures. For example, with stealing, you can avoid having to figure out whether or not he is hiding something from you by telling him he is not allowed to bring a new item into the house without a receipt. This puts you in control and eliminates arguments. Instead of listening to stories that the item was found, or a friend gave it to him or he won it in a contest, simply confiscate any new item without a receipt. It may seem unfair at times, but follow through anyway.

Cautions and Tips About Giving Extra Chores

As mentioned above, extra chores are not appropriate for children under 7 years old. Even with children 7-12 years old, make sure the extra chores you give are brief and fairly easy. With teenagers, too, limit even the toughest extra chore to no more than an hour. The important message is giving the consequence, not the severity of the chore.

🔹 Don't pick jobs that require a lot of supervision. It could end up being more of a punishment for you.

🌸 Don't give extra chores that involve the use of strong-smelling solvents. Some children will get high on inhaled fumes.

🌸 Make sure it's a job you don't care too much about, because he may not put his heart into doing it. That's why pruning your prized roses would not be a good choice. Having him write 50 things he could say instead of swear words is a better consequence. It doesn't matter if his work is sloppy. The idea is not to perfect his penmanship, but to take away his fun and freedom for a brief time.

🌸 Don't threaten to give an extra chore if he does or doesn't do something. That is a bribe. An extra chore should be given only as a consequence to a behavior.

🌸 If a child is very defiant, extra chores probably won't work. You don't want to use a strategy that adds something else to do if he already resists doing things. Remove a privilege instead. For younger children who are revved up or acting out, a time out will work better than an extra chore, because it can immediately calm the situation.

🌸 An extra chore should not be too physically demanding. Don't go overboard, for example, and make your 6-year-old move heavy rocks from one part of the yard to another. Extra chores should do no physical or long-term emotional harm.

🌸 One final note: Even when giving an extra chore, try keeping the home environment upbeat and encouraging. Just as a child won't mind being put in time out if the home atmosphere is happy, a child whose everyday life is punishing won't respond to punishment. Remember that a child will focus on the same things the parents do. Parents who concentrate on positive behavior will teach their child to get attention in a positive way.

Troubleshooting

To make any discipline effective, you must:

Be consistent.

With serious behavior especially, it's important to respond to every occurrence.

Stay calm.

Discipline works better if the focus is on the misbehavior and not the emotions surrounding it. Act before you get angry.

Stay unemotional.

If you get emotionally involved in the situation, you lose control. Don't yell or argue.

Keep it small.

Don't let things escalate and get out of control. Deal with small misbehaviors and small punishments.

Pay attention.

Act on misbehavior as soon as you notice it. Don't expect it to go away without intervening. It probably won't.

Common Problems with Discipline

I don't discipline until I'm really mad.

If you wait until you're mad, it's too late – you're reacting, not thinking.

When I get mad, I just start yelling, and my child doesn't listen.

Take time to calm down – take a deep breath, slowly count to 10 or even leave for a few minutes – then deliver the consequence in a neutral tone of voice. If you yell, he will hear your anger and not the consequence.

I often give more than one consequence.

If you're removing a privilege and sending him to his room, you could be waiting too long to act. Intervene early. Try one type of consequence at a time, increasing the severity of the consequences each time.

I find myself reacting and not knowing what I want to do.

Have a plan of action each time he misbehaves.

Sometimes it's not worth the hassle, and I let some misbehavior slide.

No one can be consistent 100% of the time. Think about the magnitude of the misbehavior and the age of the child. It's OK to let things slide every now and then. Aim for 80% consistency.

I threaten consequences, but I don't follow through enough.

Threats don't accomplish anything; discipline does.

Some Thoughts

It's easy to feel frustrated by a child's problem behavior. Think of it this way, though: Each day there are lots of times he decides to do the right thing. Take nothing for granted. Applaud him for his good decisions – it's so much easier and more pleasant than punishment.

At the same time, have confidence in your own good choices. Discipline is a tough issue, and all parents struggle with the best way to go about it. Any child must learn that there are limits. Your discipline, when done effectively, will teach him to change his behavior, so he can get along better in the world.

If the behavior continues or causes someone injury or harm, you should seek professional help. This is discussed in more detail in the next chapter.

Tips for Different Age Groups

2-6 Years
Don't use extra chores with very young children.

7-12 Years
Use extra chores that are short and not too difficult, physically or emotionally. Be as upbeat as possible. Kids probably won't like doing an extra chore, and they will be sure to tell you how they feel about it. Stay calm, and stick to your plan. Don't dwell on the behavior that earned the extra chore in the first place.

13 Years and Up
Extra chores are a good response to more serious behavior. Most teens will not want to get them. Remain pleasant and positive, and don't overreact to a behavior that seems particularly troubling because it was hidden from you. Have a backup plan that includes removing a privilege. The two strategies can work effectively hand-in-hand to change behavior.

Chapter 11

Getting Help

Sometimes you need
some roadside
assistance to
get running
and back
on the road.

When to Call for Help

What if the misbehavior won't stop, and it feels like you can't cope, as if you just don't know where to go from here? How do you know whether it's the stress of the moment or whether you need a mental health professional to help?

Wait for a calmer moment and review your situation. Ask yourself these questions:

Have you given the situation enough time to change?

It's easy to feel frustrated about disruptive behavior, but it still takes time to see real change. Give it at least a month.

Are your expectations realistic?

A child may not be ready for the kind of change you want to see. If she is relatively immature, in either her emotions or her thinking, she may need more time to learn new behavior.

Is the behavior getting worse, or is it part of a cycle of change?

It's normal for a child to rebel against change when the demand comes from a parent, her authority. It may be only temporary.

Did you really change your approach?

It may be just as hard for you to change your behavior as your child's.

If you have a circle of parent-friends, ask them to help you with these questions. If, after thinking about your situation, it looks like you need expert help, then it's time to act. Seeking help does not mean failure. Most mental health professionals will work closely with you to promote understanding and skills. If there is a serious emotional disturbance, children will need more help than a behavior modification program.

Where to Get Help

Finding the right mental health professional requires smart shopping, similar to finding any other service. The first step in any consumer choice is to gather good information. Start by talking to a trusted friend, a teacher, a minister, another parent, your pediatrician or family doctor or by calling a local mental health clinic. Look to those, especially, who have been helpful in the past.

What to Look For

Mental health professionals include counselors, social workers, ministers, psychologists or psychiatrists. All are trained experts, but not all of them will be right for you. It's important to know that your helper has experience in working with families. But just as important is whether you feel a sense of trust and comfort with your helper. Not every one will be a "good fit" for you. It's smart to try more than one before deciding.

Here are some qualities to look for in a mental health professional:

Someone who is a good listener.

A good listener gives you time enough to tell your story; and he lets you know he has heard you by paraphrasing your story. A good listener gives you the space to express your feelings. A good listener doesn't criticize or rush to advise.

Someone who explains things clearly, in language you can understand.

An expert who uses professional words without explaining their meaning may sound like an authority, but he can leave you feeling confused and overwhelmed.

Someone who gives you options, rather than directs you.

Problems usually have many possible solutions, depending on circumstances, or limitations. It feels good to know what those possibilities are, so that you can make the best choice.

Someone who recognizes that you, the parent, have the right to make choices about your child's treatment.

When you look to a professional for help, it's tempting to also give him the authority to make decisions about how to treat your child. A competent mental health professional will respect your authority to make all the decisions about your child's treatment. It's your child. It's your choice.

Someone who can develop and present a plan for treatment.

Mental health professionals are trained to assess a client's situation and come up with a plan for treatment. The treatment plan estimates the amount of time it will take, describes what the process will be, and indicates what outcomes you can expect. A plan can change, but you should know about any changes and why they were needed.

Someone who can explain issues of confidentiality.

Every state has rules that protect the confidentiality of information during treatment. Professionals should know what the rules are and be able to explain them to you. The rules are there to protect your right to privacy.

Someone who is licensed.

Ask if your counselor or therapist Is licensed. A licensed professional has met standards of training. You can call the licensing board to make sure the person is registered and in good standing.

Appendix A
Forms

1. Quick Check on Cooperation

2. Tracking Behavior

3. Behavior Contract

Quick Check on Cooperation **HOW TO USE IT**

1. Choose a time of day when you can be together with your child for about an hour straight. Try to make it a time that will be convenient for 3 days in a row.

2. During this time, make some typical requests to your child. Each time you make a request, put a mark in Request for that Day.

3. If your child started to mind within about 10 seconds after a request, then put a mark in Minded for that Day.

4. To find what percent of the time he/she minded, divide the Total for the Request by the Total for Minded.

OFF ROAD FORM

Quick Check on Cooperation

	Day 1	Day 2	Day 3
Start time:			
End time:			
Request			
Minded			

Totals

———————— / ———————— = ————————
Total request   Total minded   Percent
cooperation

Tracking Behavior   HOW TO USE IT

1. Pick a Problem behavior you want to work on. Then think of the desired opposite Positive behavior.

2. Choose a Time of Day when you can be together with your child for about an hour straight. Try to make it a time that will be convenient for 3 days in a row.

3. During each 1-hour session, observe your child's behavior in 5-10 minute periods. If you observe the problem behavior during this period, put a mark in the Problem behavior. Or, if you observe the positive behavior during this period, put a mark in the Positive behavior.

4. At the end of 3 days, add the Total count of Problem and Positive behaviors.

OFF ROAD
FORM

Tracking Behavior

1. Problem behavior_____

_____

_____

Positive behavior_____

_____

_____

2. Time of day_____

Tracking Chart

	Day 1	Day 2	Day 3	
Start time:				
End time:				**Totals**
Problem behavior				
Positive behavior				

Behavior Contract **HOW TO USE IT**

1. Fill in the child's name.
Involve younger kids by having them write their name or help you to fill in the information.

2. Choose a behavior you want to encourage.
We used the word "job" because kids can understand it better than "task" or "behavior". It helps to break a job into smaller steps, as many as you need.

3. Write down when the job needs to be finished.
Let kids know when the job needs to be done before they earn a reward.

4. Write down the number of times the job needs to be done.
Decide on a reasonable number of times kids need to do the job to earn their reward. Don't expect 100% cooperation.

5. Let kids know what reward they are working for.
A good reward motivates kids. If you're not sure what will work, find out from the kids.

6. Mark successes on a chart.
Make a chart big enough to post somewhere in the house so kids can see it. For younger children, make the chart colorful and use pictures to mark successes.

 **OFF ROAD FORM**

Behavior Contract

1. Name:_____

2. Job:_____

_____

STEPS: **a.** _____

      b. _____

      c. _____

      d. _____

      e. _____

3. When to do the job: _____

4. Number of times the job needs to be done for a reward: _____

_____

5. Reward: _____

Success Chart

Monday	Tuesday	Wednesday	Thursday	Friday	Saturday	Sunday

Appendix B
Driver's Guide for the DVD Remote

Remotes do not have common names for buttons. We chose one working name for the most important buttons. Take a moment to find out what the corresponding name is for the same button on your remote.

Important Buttons:

"MENU"
: The most important navigational button. It brings you back to the Main Menu, where you can begin choosing your path again.

"OK"
: Activates your selection.

"DIGEST"
: Goes to the Chapter Menu.

"PREV"(|<) and "NEXT"(>|)
: Skips to the previous or next choice point.

Arrow Keys
: Move the arrow on the menu screen.

"STOP"
: Stops the program.

"PAUSE"
: Pauses the action. Use the **pause** button for 2-3 minute breaks, and **stop** button for longer breaks.

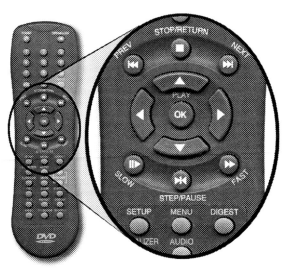

Some Things to Know About Your DVD Player

■ Follow the instructions in the DVD manual to set up your DVD player with your TV.

■ If your TV doesn't work with any of the cables that came with your DVD, talk to a Radio Shack sales person.

Appendix C
Getting Started
with the Off Road Parenting DVD

═══════════════ Overview ═══════════════

O kay, this is not your ordinary DVD. Unlike most DVD movies that give you very few choices, *Off Road Parenting* has you choose *as you watch*. This DVD is divided into "chapters" that have the same name as the chapters in the book. Each of the DVD chapters begins by having you choose which age group you want to watch. If, at any time, you want to watch a different age group, you can press the "Digest" button, select the same chapter and make a different choice.

Some chapters have "make your own story" choices. These stories have different endings depending on the choices you make. There are also question-and-answer sessions after some chapters; you select the questions and the answer plays. Chapter 3, on Tracking, has a special how-to viewing sequence.

To better understand how each chapter can be viewed, this guide has a Road Map for each chapter. The Road Map shows you the sequence of choices in the stories. If you want to go back and forth in a chapter to view other ways the story can go, the Road Map can help guide you there.

Using a DVD for parent training is a totally new self-help approach on learning parenting skills. As you will soon see, videos can't give you the variety and choices of DVDs. It's exciting! Experiment, check it out, and tell us what you think.

▬ Only for First-time DVD Viewers ▬

(Already familiar with DVDs? Skip to Chapter 1.)

Follow the directions for setting up your DVD with your TV. Place the *Off Road Parenting* DVD in the DVD player, close the disc door, and a short introduction will automatically play the Main Menu.

The Main Menu includes four options:

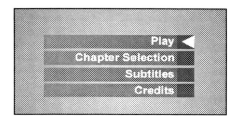

- 🦋 **Play** starts you on the journey.
- 🦋 **Chapter Selection** lets you go to a specific chapter.
- 🦋 **Subtitles** switches subtitles on or off.
- 🦋 **Credits** tells you who made this DVD.

Check that the yellow arrow on the screen is next to "Play", and then press "OK" on the remote control.

You can return to the Main Menu at any time by pressing "MENU" on the remote control.

Chapter 1: Stuck

This chapter introduces *Off Road Parenting* and also tells about some of the interactive qualities of this DVD. Your host, Dr. Rick Delaney, will invite you to choose an age group and follow a family as it travels the road to Harmony.

Select an Age Group, and press "OK".

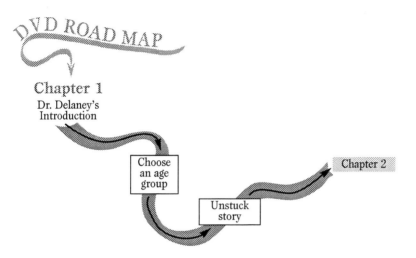

DVD ROAD MAP

Chapter 1
Dr. Delaney's
Introduction

Choose
an age
group

Unstuck
story

Chapter 2

Advanced Viewing Tip

Whenever you are watching Dr. Delaney's comments at the end of a scene, you can press the "PREV"(|<) button on your remote before he finishes his comments, to return to the previous choice point. This allows you to explore another path.

Chapter 2: Cooperation

Chapter 2 shows how to make an effective request.

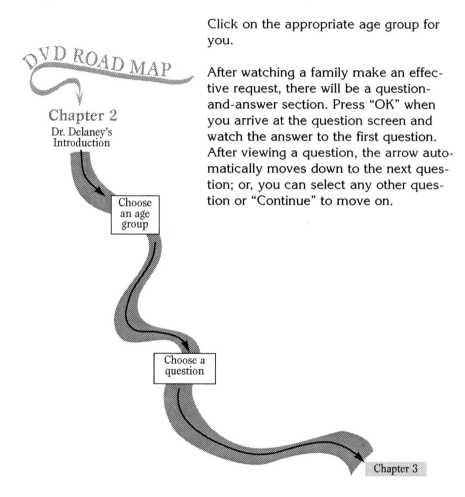

Click on the appropriate age group for you.

After watching a family make an effective request, there will be a question-and-answer section. Press "OK" when you arrive at the question screen and watch the answer to the first question. After viewing a question, the arrow automatically moves down to the next question; or, you can select any other question or "Continue" to move on.

Chapter 3: Tracking

Chapter 3 helps you get a clear understanding of what Tracking is and how to use it.

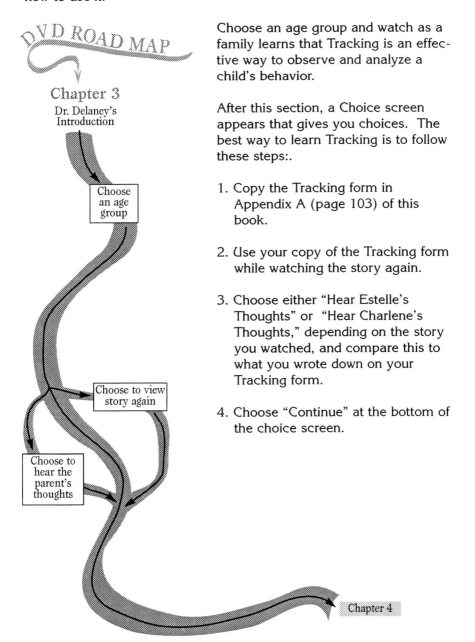

Choose an age group and watch as a family learns that Tracking is an effective way to observe and analyze a child's behavior.

After this section, a Choice screen appears that gives you choices. The best way to learn Tracking is to follow these steps:.

1. Copy the Tracking form in Appendix A (page 103) of this book.

2. Use your copy of the Tracking form while watching the story again.

3. Choose either "Hear Estelle's Thoughts" or "Hear Charlene's Thoughts," depending on the story you watched, and compare this to what you wrote down on your Tracking form.

4. Choose "Continue" at the bottom of the choice screen.

Chapter 4: Encouragement

Chapter 4 is on encouraging positive behavior.

There are no special viewing techniques with this chapter.

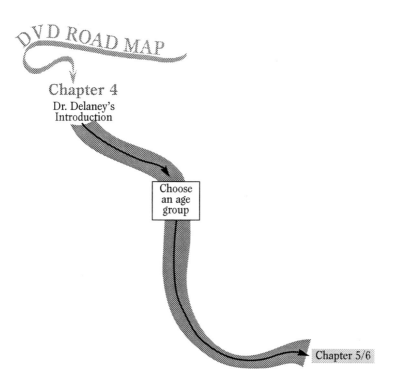

Chapter 5/6: Behavior Contracts

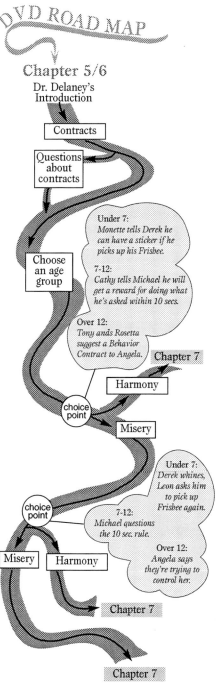

DVD ROAD MAP

Chapter 5/6

Dr. Delaney's
Introduction

Contracts

Questions
about
contracts

Choose
an age
group

Under 7:
*Monette tells Derek he
can have a sticker if he
picks up his Frisbee.*

7-12:
*Cathy tells Michael he will
get a reward for doing what
he's asked within 10 secs.*

Over 12:
*Tony and Rosetta
suggest a Behavior
Contract to Angela.* Chapter 7

Harmony

choice
point

Misery

Under 7:
*Derek whines,
Leon asks him
to pick up
Frisbee again.*

choice
point

7-12:
*Michael questions
the 10 sec. rule.*

Misery   Harmony

Over 12:
*Angela says
they're trying to
control her.*

Chapter 7

Chapter 7

Chapter 5/6 describes what a Behavior Contract is and how to use it.

In the first section, watch as one family encounters a problem behavior with their teen and decides to use a Behavior Contract.

The second section is an interactive Behavior Contract. Press "OK" when you arrive at the contract screen and learn more about the first section. When you return to the contract screen, the arrow automatically moves down to the next section. Press "OK", or select another section.

Select "Continue" at any point to move on to the third section of this chapter.

The third section of Chapter 5/6 is about how to approach kids with Behavior Contracts and get them involved.

Choose an age group and watch parents present the idea of a Behavior Contract to their kids.

There are two choice screens in each story that will affect what happens. Choose between the road to Harmony or Misery, and the child in the family either accepts or rejects the Behavior Contract

Start by pressing the "OK" button at each choice point to see our suggested viewing sequence.

Exploring Another Path

Choose the "DIGEST" button to return to the Chapter Menu; select Chapter 5/6, and press "OK" to view it again. Now press the "NEXT"(>|) button until you arrive at the choice point you wanted; then make your new choice.

You can also jump forward or backward between choice points by selecting the appropriate "Previous Choice" or "Next Choice" buttons on the Choice screen.

Chapter 7:

Chapter 7 deals with establishing house rules as a way of Setting Limits.

Choose from three stories on how different families use house rules with their kids. This time the stories show kids at different ages, and consider whether they are new to, or already living in, the home.

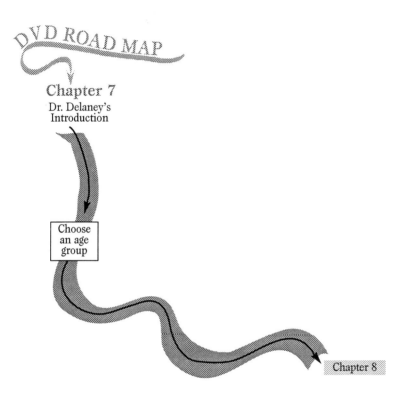

DVD ROAD MAP

Chapter 7
Dr. Delaney's
Introduction

Choose
an age
group

Chapter 8

Chapter 8

Chapter 8 shows how parents use Time Out with children under 12 years old.

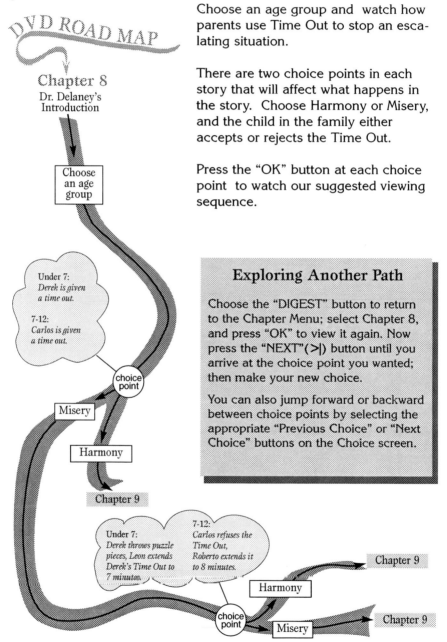

DVD ROAD MAP

Chapter 8
Dr. Delaney's
Introduction

Choose
an age
group

Under 7:
Derek is given
a time out.

7-12:
Carlos is given
a time out.

choice point

Misery

Harmony

Chapter 9

Under 7:
Derek throws puzzle
pieces, Leon extends
Derek's Time Out to
7 minutes.

7-12:
Carlos refuses the
Time Out,
Roberto extends it
to 8 minutes.

choice point

Harmony

Misery

Chapter 9

Chapter 9

Choose an age group and watch how parents use Time Out to stop an escalating situation.

There are two choice points in each story that will affect what happens in the story. Choose Harmony or Misery, and the child in the family either accepts or rejects the Time Out.

Press the "OK" button at each choice point to watch our suggested viewing sequence.

Exploring Another Path

Choose the "DIGEST" button to return to the Chapter Menu; select Chapter 8, and press "OK" to view it again. Now press the "NEXT"(>|) button until you arrive at the choice point you wanted; then make your new choice.

You can also jump forward or backward between choice points by selecting the appropriate "Previous Choice" or "Next Choice" buttons on the Choice screen.

Chapter 9

Chapter 9 explains Privilege Removal and how it can be a powerful tool for parents.

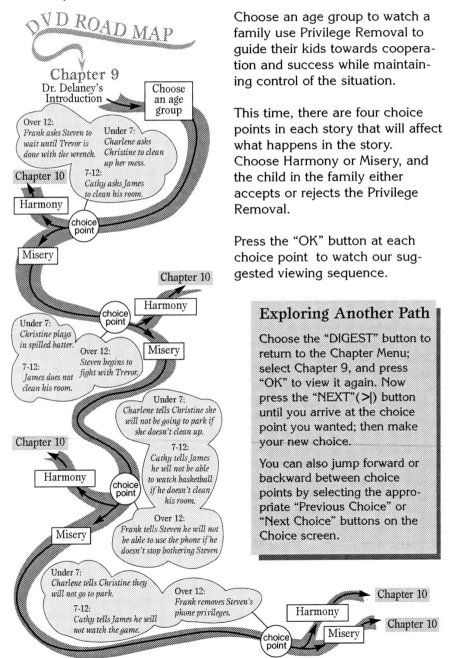

DVD ROAD MAP

Chapter 9
Dr. Delaney's Introduction

Choose an age group

Over 12:
Frank asks Steven to wait until Trevor is done with the wrench.

Under 7:
Charlene asks Christine to clean up her mess.

Chapter 10

7-12:
Cathy asks James to clean his room.

Harmony

choice point

Misery

Chapter 10

choice point

Harmony

Under 7:
Christine plays in spilled batter.

Over 12:
Steven begins to fight with Trevor.

Misery

7-12:
James does not clean his room.

Under 7:
Charlene tells Christine she will not be going to park if she doesn't clean up.

Chapter 10

7-12:
Cathy tells James he will not be able to watch basketball if he doesn't clean his room.

Harmony

choice point

Misery

Over 12:
Frank tells Steven he will not be able to use the phone if he doesn't stop bothering Steven

Under 7:
Charlene tells Christine they will not go to park.

7-12:
Cathy tells James he will not watch the game.

Over 12:
Frank removes Steven's phone privileges.

Harmony

Chapter 10

choice point

Misery

Chapter 10

Choose an age group to watch a family use Privilege Removal to guide their kids towards cooperation and success while maintaining control of the situation.

This time, there are four choice points in each story that will affect what happens in the story. Choose Harmony or Misery, and the child in the family either accepts or rejects the Privilege Removal.

Press the "OK" button at each choice point to watch our suggested viewing sequence.

Exploring Another Path

Choose the "DIGEST" button to return to the Chapter Menu; select Chapter 9, and press "OK" to view it again. Now press the "NEXT" (>|) button until you arrive at the choice point you wanted; then make your new choice.

You can also jump forward or backward between choice points by selecting the appropriate "Previous Choice" or "Next Choice" buttons on the Choice screen.

Chapter 10

Chapter 10 shows how to use Extra Chores as an effective parenting tool.

Watch how one family gives an Extra Chore to their teen when dealing with a difficult situation.

There are two choice points in the story that will affect what happens. Choose Harmony or Misery, and the child in the family either accepts or rejects the Extra Chore.

Press the "OK" button at each choice point to watch our suggested viewing sequence.

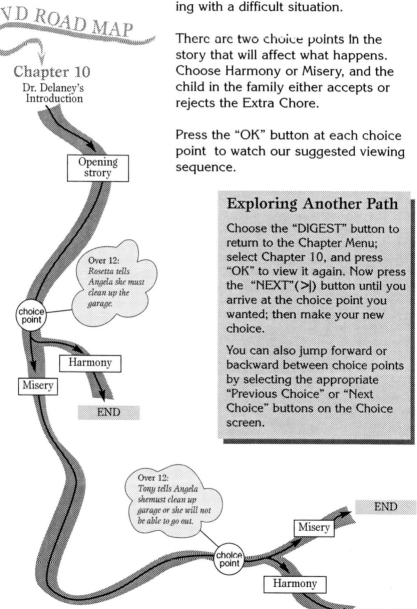

Exploring Another Path

Choose the "DIGEST" button to return to the Chapter Menu; select Chapter 10, and press "OK" to view it again. Now press the "NEXT"(>|) button until you arrive at the choice point you wanted; then make your new choice.

You can also jump forward or backward between choice points by selecting the appropriate "Previous Choice" or "Next Choice" buttons on the Choice screen.

DVD ROAD MAP

Chapter 10
Dr. Delaney's Introduction

Opening strory

Over 12:
Rosetta tells Angela she must clean up the garage.

choice point

Harmony

Misery

END

Over 12:
Tony tells Angela she must clean up garage or she will not be able to go out.

choice point

Misery

END

Harmony

END

About the Contributors

Caesar Pacifici, Ph.D., an educational psychologist specializing in child development, received his doctorate from the City University of New York. As a partner and Director of Research at Northwest Media, his work focuses on using emerging media technology for teaching social learning to at-risk kids and parents. He has designed multimedia and Web-based curricula on daily living skills, the prevention of coercive sexual behavior, parenting, and caring for elders. Dr. Pacifici is a licensed psychologist in Oregon and works with young adults in his practice.

Patricia Chamberlain, Ph.D., is the Clinical Director of Oregon Social Learning Center, a nationally acclaimed research group focusing on family, peer group and school experiences. Her work centers on developing and testing treatment methods for kids and families who are dealing with delinquency and conduct problems. She is also a well-known researcher in the area of Treatment Foster Care, a program for foster parent training and therapy.

Lee White has plenty of firsthand experience with the demands of parenting. Raised in the post-World War II era by a single, working mother, he was a latchkey kid before the term was invented. As a young adult and single parent, he struggled to raise two boys with no backup support and scant financial means. Now happily married — and his boys all grown up — he and his wife are "kinship parents" to a teen and have been surrogate parents to a number of foreign students. Mr. White is president of Northwest Media, a company devoted to social learning and helping families and youth. He authored *The Teenage Human Body Operator's Manual* and has produced numerous foster care and independent-living training materials that he presents at training conferences

Jan Eliot is the creator of the syndicated cartoon strip *Stone Soup*, which appears in more than 130 papers in the United States, Canada, and Europe. She has also published two collections of her work, *You Can't Say Boobs on Sunday* and *Stone Soup the Comic Strip*. Ms. Eliot lives in Eugene, Oregon, where as a young, single mother she began cartooning as a counterpoint to having too little patience, time and money. She hopes her cartoons, which come from her own experiences, provide comic relief for parents and kids everywhere.

Jan's books are available at bookstores and on www.LotsofLearning.com

You Can't Say
Boobs on Sunday
ISBN: 0-9674102-1-7

Stone Soup
The Comic Strip
ISBN: 0-9674102-1-5

About the DVD Contributors

Carrie Keller graduated with a degree in communication arts from the University of Wisconsin, Madison. Ms. Keller brought ten years of production experience to her position as media director at Northwest Media, where she writes, produces and directs the company's educational videos and DVDs. Her interest in social issues comes from her experience as the child of divorced parents as well as her work with Head Start and Circle of Discipline, a boxing program designed to provide kids with an alternative to street violence.

Dr. Richard J. Delaney, narrator of the *Off Road Parenting* DVD, is a nationally known trainer and consultant who has worked extensively with troubled children and youth since 1970. He has consulted to foster and adoptive parents, caseworkers, mental health professionals and child care agencies over the past 25 years. Dr. Delaney received his Ph.D. in clinical psychology from Loyola University of Chicago in 1973. He is a licensed psychologist in Colorado and Hawaii. Dr. Delaney is a father and stepfather and lives in Grand Junction, Colorado.

DVD Production Credits

Project Director
Caesar Pacifici, Ph.D.

Executive Producer
Lee White

Content Director
Carrie Keller

Video Producer
Chambers Productions
Tracy Berry

Director
Chambers Productions
Steve Ogle

Multimedia Producer
Carrie Keller

Multimedia Interactive Design
Lee White
Carrie Keller
Caesar Pacifici, Ph.D.

Scriptwriters
Carrie Keller
Lee White
Caesar Pacifici, Ph.D.

Script Consultants
Patricia Chamberlain, Ph.D.
J.P. Davis
Carla Antoine
Holly Graham

Graphic Design
Diane Cissel

Video Production
Chambers Productions and
Northwest Media, Inc.

DVD Authoring
Acutrack, Inc.

Off Road Parenting was funded by the Small Business Innovative Research Program through a grant from the National Institute of Mental Health to Northwest Media, Inc., Project #R44 MH 52028.